Date:

_____

"Little by little we let go of loss but never of love."

Something that reminded me of you today:

_____

_____

_____

_____

Today I wish I could tell you:

_____

_____

_____

_____

I am grateful for the time:

_____

_____

_____

_____

The most difficult time of today:

_____

_____

_____

_____

Date:

_____

"Little by little we let go of loss but never of love."

Something that reminded me of you today:

_____

_____

_____

_____

Today I wish I could tell you:

_____

_____

_____

_____

I am grateful for the time:

_____

_____

_____

_____

The most difficult time of today:

_____

_____

_____

_____

Date:

_____

"Little by little we let go of loss but never of love."

Something that reminded me of you today:

_____

_____

_____

_____

_____

Today I wish I could tell you:

_____

_____

_____

_____

_____

I am grateful for the time:

_____

_____

_____

_____

_____

The most difficult time of today:

_____

_____

_____

_____

Date:

_____

"Little by little we let go of loss but never of love."

Something that reminded me of you today:

_____

_____

_____

_____

Today I wish I could tell you:

_____

_____

_____

_____

I am grateful for the time:

_____

_____

_____

_____

The most difficult time of today:

_____

_____

_____

Date:

_____

"Little by little we let go of loss but never of love."

Something that reminded me of you today:

_____

_____

_____

_____

Today I wish I could tell you:

_____

_____

_____

_____

_____

I am grateful for the time:

_____

_____

_____

_____

_____

The most difficult time of today:

_____

_____

_____

_____

Date:

_____

"Little by little we let go of loss but never of love."

Something that reminded me of you today:

_____

_____

_____

_____

Today I wish I could tell you:

_____

_____

_____

_____

I am grateful for the time:

_____

_____

_____

_____

The most difficult time of today:

_____

_____

_____

Date:
_____

"Little by little we let go of loss but never of love."

Something that reminded me of you today:

_____
_____
_____
_____

Today I wish I could tell you:

_____
_____
_____
_____

I am grateful for the time:

_____
_____
_____
_____

The most difficult time of today:

_____
_____
_____

Date:

_____

"Little by little we let go of loss but never of love."

Something that reminded me of you today:

_____
_____
_____
_____

Today I wish I could tell you:

_____
_____
_____
_____

I am grateful for the time:

_____
_____
_____
_____

The most difficult time of today:

_____
_____
_____

Date:

_____

"Little by little we let go of loss but never of love."

Something that reminded me of you today:

_____

_____

_____

_____

Today I wish I could tell you:

_____

_____

_____

_____

I am grateful for the time:

_____

_____

_____

_____

The most difficult time of today:

_____

_____

_____

_____

Date:

_____

"Little by little we let go of loss but never of love."

Something that reminded me of you today:

_____

_____

_____

_____

Today I wish I could tell you:

_____

_____

_____

_____

I am grateful for the time:

_____

_____

_____

_____

The most difficult time of today:

_____

_____

_____

_____

Date:

_____

"Little by little we let go of loss but never of love."

Something that reminded me of you today:

_____

_____

_____

_____

Today I wish I could tell you:

_____

_____

_____

_____

I am grateful for the time:

_____

_____

_____

_____

The most difficult time of today:

_____

_____

_____

_____

Date:

_____

"Little by little we let go of loss but never of love."

Something that reminded me of you today:

_____

_____

_____

_____

Today I wish I could tell you:

_____

_____

_____

_____

I am grateful for the time:

_____

_____

_____

_____

The most difficult time of today:

_____

_____

_____

_____

Date:

_____

"Little by little we let go of loss but never of love."

Something that reminded me of you today:

_____
_____
_____
_____
_____

Today I wish I could tell you:

_____
_____
_____
_____
_____

I am grateful for the time:

_____
_____
_____
_____
_____

The most difficult time of today:

_____
_____
_____
_____

Date:

_____

"Little by little we let go of loss but never of love."

Something that reminded me of you today:

_____

_____

_____

_____

Today I wish I could tell you:

_____

_____

_____

_____

I am grateful for the time:

_____

_____

_____

_____

The most difficult time of today:

_____

_____

_____

Date:

_____

"Little by little we let go of loss but never of love."

Something that reminded me of you today:

_____

_____

_____

_____

Today I wish I could tell you:

_____

_____

_____

_____

I am grateful for the time:

_____

_____

_____

_____

The most difficult time of today:

_____

_____

_____

Date:

_____

"Little by little we let go of loss but never of love."

Something that reminded me of you today:

_____

_____

_____

_____

Today I wish I could tell you:

_____

_____

_____

_____

I am grateful for the time:

_____

_____

_____

_____

The most difficult time of today:

_____

_____

_____

Date:

_____

"Little by little we let go of loss but never of love."

Something that reminded me of you today:

_____
_____
_____
_____
_____

Today I wish I could tell you:

_____
_____
_____
_____
_____

I am grateful for the time:

_____
_____
_____
_____
_____

The most difficult time of today:

_____
_____
_____
_____

Date:

_____

"Little by little we let go of loss but never of love."

Something that reminded me of you today:

_____

_____

_____

_____

Today I wish I could tell you:

_____

_____

_____

_____

I am grateful for the time:

_____

_____

_____

_____

The most difficult time of today:

_____

_____

_____

_____

Date:

_____

"Little by little we let go of loss but never of love."

Something that reminded me of you today:

_____
_____
_____
_____
_____

Today I wish I could tell you:

_____
_____
_____
_____
_____

I am grateful for the time:

_____
_____
_____
_____
_____

The most difficult time of today:

_____
_____
_____
_____

Date:

_____

"Little by little we let go of loss but never of love."

Something that reminded me of you today:

_____

_____

_____

_____

Today I wish I could tell you:

_____

_____

_____

_____

I am grateful for the time:

_____

_____

_____

_____

The most difficult time of today:

_____

_____

_____

Date:
_____

"Little by little we let go of loss but never of love."

Something that reminded me of you today:

_____
_____
_____
_____
_____

Today I wish I could tell you:

_____
_____
_____
_____
_____

I am grateful for the time:

_____
_____
_____
_____
_____

The most difficult time of today:

_____
_____
_____
_____

Date:

_____

"Little by little we let go of loss but never of love."

Something that reminded me of you today:

_____
_____
_____
_____
_____

Today I wish I could tell you:

_____
_____
_____
_____
_____

I am grateful for the time:

_____
_____
_____
_____
_____

The most difficult time of today:

_____
_____
_____
_____

Date:

_____

"Little by little we let go of loss but never of love."

Something that reminded me of you today:

_____

_____

_____

_____

Today I wish I could tell you:

_____

_____

_____

_____

I am grateful for the time:

_____

_____

_____

_____

The most difficult time of today:

_____

_____

_____

Date:

_____

"Little by little we let go of loss but never of love."

Something that reminded me of you today:

_____

_____

_____

_____

Today I wish I could tell you:

_____

_____

_____

_____

I am grateful for the time:

_____

_____

_____

_____

The most difficult time of today:

_____

_____

_____

_____

Date:

_____

"Little by little we let go of loss but never of love."

Something that reminded me of you today:

_____
_____
_____
_____
_____

Today I wish I could tell you:

_____
_____
_____
_____
_____

I am grateful for the time:

_____
_____
_____
_____
_____

The most difficult time of today:

_____
_____
_____
_____

Date:

_____

"Little by little we let go of loss but never of love."

Something that reminded me of you today:

_____

_____

_____

_____

Today I wish I could tell you:

_____

_____

_____

_____

I am grateful for the time:

_____

_____

_____

_____

The most difficult time of today:

_____

_____

_____

_____

Date:

_____

"Little by little we let go of loss but never of love."

Something that reminded me of you today:

_____

_____

_____

_____

_____

Today I wish I could tell you:

_____

_____

_____

_____

_____

I am grateful for the time:

_____

_____

_____

_____

_____

The most difficult time of today:

_____

_____

_____

_____

Date:
_____

"Little by little we let go of loss but never of love."

Something that reminded me of you today:

_____
_____
_____
_____

Today I wish I could tell you:

_____
_____
_____
_____

I am grateful for the time:

_____
_____
_____
_____

The most difficult time of today:

_____
_____
_____

Date:

_____

"Little by little we let go of loss but never of love."

Something that reminded me of you today:

_____

_____

_____

_____

Today I wish I could tell you:

_____

_____

_____

_____

I am grateful for the time:

_____

_____

_____

_____

The most difficult time of today:

_____

_____

_____

_____

Date:

_____

"Little by little we let go of loss but never of love."

Something that reminded me of you today:

_____

_____

_____

_____

Today I wish I could tell you:

_____

_____

_____

_____

I am grateful for the time:

_____

_____

_____

_____

The most difficult time of today:

_____

_____

_____

_____

Date:

_____

"Little by little we let go of loss but never of love."

Something that reminded me of you today:

_____

_____

_____

_____

_____

Today I wish I could tell you:

_____

_____

_____

_____

_____

I am grateful for the time:

_____

_____

_____

_____

_____

The most difficult time of today:

_____

_____

_____

_____

Date:

_____

"Little by little we let go of loss but never of love."

Something that reminded me of you today:

_____
_____
_____
_____

Today I wish I could tell you:

_____
_____
_____
_____

I am grateful for the time:

_____
_____
_____
_____

The most difficult time of today:

_____
_____
_____
_____

Date:

_____

"Little by little we let go of loss but never of love."

Something that reminded me of you today:

_____

_____

_____

_____

Today I wish I could tell you:

_____

_____

_____

_____

I am grateful for the time:

_____

_____

_____

_____

The most difficult time of today:

_____

_____

_____

Date:

_____

"Little by little we let go of loss but never of love."

Something that reminded me of you today:

_____

_____

_____

_____

Today I wish I could tell you:

_____

_____

_____

_____

I am grateful for the time:

_____

_____

_____

_____

The most difficult time of today:

_____

_____

_____

_____

Date:

_____

"Little by little we let go of loss but never of love."

Something that reminded me of you today:

_____
_____
_____
_____

Today I wish I could tell you:

_____
_____
_____
_____

I am grateful for the time:

_____
_____
_____
_____

The most difficult time of today:

_____
_____
_____

Date:

_____

"Little by little we let go of loss but never of love."

Something that reminded me of you today:

_____

_____

_____

_____

Today I wish I could tell you:

_____

_____

_____

_____

I am grateful for the time:

_____

_____

_____

_____

The most difficult time of today:

_____

_____

_____

_____

Date:

_____

"Little by little we let go of loss but never of love."

Something that reminded me of you today:

_____

_____

_____

_____

Today I wish I could tell you:

_____

_____

_____

_____

I am grateful for the time:

_____

_____

_____

_____

The most difficult time of today:

_____

_____

_____

_____

Date:

_____

"Little by little we let go of loss but never of love."

Something that reminded me of you today:

_____
_____
_____
_____
_____

Today I wish I could tell you:

_____
_____
_____
_____
_____

I am grateful for the time:

_____
_____
_____
_____
_____

The most difficult time of today:

_____
_____
_____
_____

Date:

_____

"Little by little we let go of loss but never of love."

Something that reminded me of you today:

_____

_____

_____

_____

Today I wish I could tell you:

_____

_____

_____

_____

I am grateful for the time:

_____

_____

_____

_____

The most difficult time of today:

_____

_____

_____

Date:
_____

"Little by little we let go of loss but never of love."

Something that reminded me of you today:

_____
_____
_____
_____

Today I wish I could tell you:

_____
_____
_____
_____

I am grateful for the time:

_____
_____
_____
_____

The most difficult time of today:

_____
_____
_____
_____

Date:

_____

"Little by little we let go of loss but never of love."

Something that reminded me of you today:

_____
_____
_____
_____

Today I wish I could tell you:

_____
_____
_____
_____

I am grateful for the time:

_____
_____
_____
_____

The most difficult time of today:

_____
_____
_____
_____

Date:

_____

"Little by little we let go of loss but never of love."

Something that reminded me of you today:

_____

_____

_____

_____

Today I wish I could tell you:

_____

_____

_____

_____

I am grateful for the time:

_____

_____

_____

_____

The most difficult time of today:

_____

_____

_____

Date:

_____

"Little by little we let go of loss but never of love."

Something that reminded me of you today:

_____

_____

_____

_____

Today I wish I could tell you:

_____

_____

_____

_____

I am grateful for the time:

_____

_____

_____

_____

The most difficult time of today:

_____

_____

_____

_____

Date:

_____

"Little by little we let go of loss but never of love."

Something that reminded me of you today:

_____

_____

_____

_____

Today I wish I could tell you:

_____

_____

_____

_____

I am grateful for the time:

_____

_____

_____

_____

The most difficult time of today:

_____

_____

_____

_____

Date:

_____

"Little by little we let go of loss but never of love."

Something that reminded me of you today:

_____

_____

_____

_____

Today I wish I could tell you:

_____

_____

_____

_____

I am grateful for the time:

_____

_____

_____

_____

The most difficult time of today:

_____

_____

_____

_____

Date:

_____

"Little by little we let go of loss but never of love."

Something that reminded me of you today:

_____

_____

_____

_____

_____

Today I wish I could tell you:

_____

_____

_____

_____

_____

I am grateful for the time:

_____

_____

_____

_____

_____

The most difficult time of today:

_____

_____

_____

_____

Date:

_____

"Little by little we let go of loss but never of love."

Something that reminded me of you today:

_____

_____

_____

_____

Today I wish I could tell you:

_____

_____

_____

_____

I am grateful for the time:

_____

_____

_____

_____

The most difficult time of today:

_____

_____

_____

Date:

_____

"Little by little we let go of loss but never of love."

Something that reminded me of you today:

_____

_____

_____

_____

Today I wish I could tell you:

_____

_____

_____

_____

I am grateful for the time:

_____

_____

_____

_____

The most difficult time of today:

_____

_____

_____

_____

Date:

_____

"Little by little we let go of loss but never of love."

Something that reminded me of you today:

_____
_____
_____
_____

Today I wish I could tell you:

_____
_____
_____
_____

I am grateful for the time:

_____
_____
_____
_____

The most difficult time of today:

_____
_____
_____
_____

Date:

_____

"Little by little we let go of loss but never of love."

Something that reminded me of you today:

_____

_____

_____

_____

Today I wish I could tell you:

_____

_____

_____

_____

I am grateful for the time:

_____

_____

_____

_____

The most difficult time of today:

_____

_____

_____

_____

Date:
_____

"Little by little we let go of loss but never of love."

Something that reminded me of you today:

_____
_____
_____
_____

Today I wish I could tell you:

_____
_____
_____
_____

I am grateful for the time:

_____
_____
_____
_____

The most difficult time of today:

_____
_____
_____

Date:

_____

"Little by little we let go of loss but never of love."

Something that reminded me of you today:

_____
_____
_____
_____
_____

Today I wish I could tell you:

_____
_____
_____
_____
_____

I am grateful for the time:

_____
_____
_____
_____
_____

The most difficult time of today:

_____
_____
_____
_____

Date:

_____

"Little by little we let go of loss but never of love."

Something that reminded me of you today:

_____

_____

_____

_____

_____

Today I wish I could tell you:

_____

_____

_____

_____

_____

I am grateful for the time:

_____

_____

_____

_____

_____

The most difficult time of today:

_____

_____

_____

_____

Date:

_____

"Little by little we let go of loss but never of love."

Something that reminded me of you today:

_____

_____

_____

_____

Today I wish I could tell you:

_____

_____

_____

_____

I am grateful for the time:

_____

_____

_____

_____

The most difficult time of today:

_____

_____

_____

_____

Date:

_____

"Little by little we let go of loss but never of love."

Something that reminded me of you today:

_____

_____

_____

_____

Today I wish I could tell you:

_____

_____

_____

_____

I am grateful for the time:

_____

_____

_____

_____

The most difficult time of today:

_____

_____

_____

Date:

_____

"Little by little we let go of loss but never of love."

Something that reminded me of you today:

_____

_____

_____

_____

Today I wish I could tell you:

_____

_____

_____

_____

I am grateful for the time:

_____

_____

_____

_____

The most difficult time of today:

_____

_____

_____

_____

Date:

_____

"Little by little we let go of loss but never of love."

Something that reminded me of you today:

_____

_____

_____

_____

Today I wish I could tell you:

_____

_____

_____

_____

I am grateful for the time:

_____

_____

_____

_____

The most difficult time of today:

_____

_____

_____

_____

Date:

_____

"Little by little we let go of loss but never of love."

Something that reminded me of you today:

_____

_____

_____

_____

Today I wish I could tell you:

_____

_____

_____

_____

I am grateful for the time:

_____

_____

_____

_____

The most difficult time of today:

_____

_____

_____

_____

Date:

_____

"Little by little we let go of loss but never of love."

Something that reminded me of you today:

_____
_____
_____
_____

Today I wish I could tell you:

_____
_____
_____
_____

I am grateful for the time:

_____
_____
_____
_____

The most difficult time of today:

_____
_____
_____

Date:

_____

"Little by little we let go of loss but never of love."

Something that reminded me of you today:

_____

_____

_____

_____

Today I wish I could tell you:

_____

_____

_____

_____

I am grateful for the time:

_____

_____

_____

_____

The most difficult time of today:

_____

_____

_____

_____

Date:

_____

"Little by little we let go of loss but never of love."

Something that reminded me of you today:

_____
_____
_____
_____

Today I wish I could tell you:

_____
_____
_____
_____

I am grateful for the time:

_____
_____
_____
_____

The most difficult time of today:

_____
_____
_____
_____

Date:

_____

"Little by little we let go of loss but never of love."

Something that reminded me of you today:

_____
_____
_____
_____

Today I wish I could tell you:

_____
_____
_____
_____

I am grateful for the time:

_____
_____
_____
_____

The most difficult time of today:

_____
_____
_____
_____

Date:

_____

"Little by little we let go of loss but never of love."

Something that reminded me of you today:

_____

_____

_____

_____

Today I wish I could tell you:

_____

_____

_____

_____

I am grateful for the time:

_____

_____

_____

_____

The most difficult time of today:

_____

_____

_____

Date:

_____

"Little by little we let go of loss but never of love."

Something that reminded me of you today:

_____

_____

_____

_____

Today I wish I could tell you:

_____

_____

_____

_____

I am grateful for the time:

_____

_____

_____

_____

The most difficult time of today:

_____

_____

_____

_____

Date:

_____

"Little by little we let go of loss but never of love."

Something that reminded me of you today:

_____

_____

_____

_____

Today I wish I could tell you:

_____

_____

_____

_____

I am grateful for the time:

_____

_____

_____

_____

The most difficult time of today:

_____

_____

_____

_____

Date:

_____

"Little by little we let go of loss but never of love."

Something that reminded me of you today:

_____

_____

_____

_____

Today I wish I could tell you:

_____

_____

_____

_____

I am grateful for the time:

_____

_____

_____

_____

The most difficult time of today:

_____

_____

_____

_____

Date:

_____

"Little by little we let go of loss but never of love."

Something that reminded me of you today:

_____
_____
_____
_____

Today I wish I could tell you:

_____
_____
_____
_____

I am grateful for the time:

_____
_____
_____
_____

The most difficult time of today:

_____
_____
_____
_____

Date:

_____

"Little by little we let go of loss but never of love."

Something that reminded me of you today:

_____

_____

_____

_____

Today I wish I could tell you:

_____

_____

_____

_____

I am grateful for the time:

_____

_____

_____

_____

The most difficult time of today:

_____

_____

_____

_____

Date:

_____

"Little by little we let go of loss but never of love."

Something that reminded me of you today:

_____

_____

_____

_____

Today I wish I could tell you:

_____

_____

_____

_____

I am grateful for the time:

_____

_____

_____

_____

The most difficult time of today:

_____

_____

_____

Date:

_____

"Little by little we let go of loss but never of love."

Something that reminded me of you today:

_____

_____

_____

_____

Today I wish I could tell you:

_____

_____

_____

_____

I am grateful for the time:

_____

_____

_____

_____

The most difficult time of today:

_____

_____

_____

Date:

_____

"Little by little we let go of loss but never of love."

Something that reminded me of you today:

_____

_____

_____

_____

Today I wish I could tell you:

_____

_____

_____

_____

I am grateful for the time:

_____

_____

_____

_____

The most difficult time of today:

_____

_____

_____

_____

Date:

_____

"Little by little we let go of loss but never of love."

Something that reminded me of you today:

_____

_____

_____

_____

Today I wish I could tell you:

_____

_____

_____

_____

I am grateful for the time:

_____

_____

_____

_____

The most difficult time of today:

_____

_____

_____

Date:
_____

"Little by little we let go of loss but never of love."

Something that reminded me of you today:

_____
_____
_____
_____

Today I wish I could tell you:

_____
_____
_____
_____

I am grateful for the time:

_____
_____
_____
_____

The most difficult time of today:

_____
_____
_____
_____

Date:

_____

"Little by little we let go of loss but never of love."

Something that reminded me of you today:

_____
_____
_____
_____

Today I wish I could tell you:

_____
_____
_____
_____

I am grateful for the time:

_____
_____
_____
_____

The most difficult time of today:

_____
_____
_____
_____

Date:

_____

"Little by little we let go of loss but never of love."

Something that reminded me of you today:

_____
_____
_____
_____
_____

Today I wish I could tell you:

_____
_____
_____
_____
_____

I am grateful for the time:

_____
_____
_____
_____
_____

The most difficult time of today:

_____
_____
_____
_____

Date:

_____

"Little by little we let go of loss but never of love."

Something that reminded me of you today:

_____

_____

_____

_____

Today I wish I could tell you:

_____

_____

_____

_____

I am grateful for the time:

_____

_____

_____

_____

The most difficult time of today:

_____

_____

_____

_____

Date:

_____

"Little by little we let go of loss but never of love."

Something that reminded me of you today:

_____
_____
_____
_____
_____

Today I wish I could tell you:

_____
_____
_____
_____
_____

I am grateful for the time:

_____
_____
_____
_____

The most difficult time of today:

_____
_____
_____
_____

Date:

_____

"Little by little we let go of loss but never of love."

Something that reminded me of you today:

_____

_____

_____

_____

Today I wish I could tell you:

_____

_____

_____

_____

I am grateful for the time:

_____

_____

_____

_____

The most difficult time of today:

_____

_____

_____

Date:

_____

"Little by little we let go of loss but never of love."

Something that reminded me of you today:

_____

_____

_____

_____

Today I wish I could tell you:

_____

_____

_____

_____

I am grateful for the time:

_____

_____

_____

_____

The most difficult time of today:

_____

_____

_____

_____

Date:

_____

"Little by little we let go of loss but never of love."

Something that reminded me of you today:

_____

_____

_____

_____

Today I wish I could tell you:

_____

_____

_____

_____

I am grateful for the time:

_____

_____

_____

_____

The most difficult time of today:

_____

_____

_____

_____

Date:
_____

"Little by little we let go of loss but never of love."

Something that reminded me of you today:

_____
_____
_____
_____
_____

Today I wish I could tell you:

_____
_____
_____
_____
_____

I am grateful for the time:

_____
_____
_____
_____
_____

The most difficult time of today:

_____
_____
_____
_____

Date:

_____

"Little by little we let go of loss but never of love."

Something that reminded me of you today:

_____

_____

_____

_____

Today I wish I could tell you:

_____

_____

_____

_____

I am grateful for the time:

_____

_____

_____

_____

The most difficult time of today:

_____

_____

_____

_____

Date:

_____

"Little by little we let go of loss but never of love."

Something that reminded me of you today:

_____
_____
_____
_____
_____

Today I wish I could tell you:

_____
_____
_____
_____
_____

I am grateful for the time:

_____
_____
_____
_____
_____

The most difficult time of today:

_____
_____
_____
_____

Date:

_____

"Little by little we let go of loss but never of love."

Something that reminded me of you today:

_____
_____
_____
_____

Today I wish I could tell you:

_____
_____
_____
_____

I am grateful for the time:

_____
_____
_____
_____

The most difficult time of today:

_____
_____
_____

Date:

_____

"Little by little we let go of loss but never of love."

Something that reminded me of you today:

_____

_____

_____

_____

Today I wish I could tell you:

_____

_____

_____

_____

I am grateful for the time:

_____

_____

_____

_____

The most difficult time of today:

_____

_____

_____

Date:

_____

"Little by little we let go of loss but never of love."

Something that reminded me of you today:

_____
_____
_____
_____

Today I wish I could tell you:

_____
_____
_____
_____

I am grateful for the time:

_____
_____
_____
_____

The most difficult time of today:

_____
_____
_____

Date:

_____

"Little by little we let go of loss but never of love."

Something that reminded me of you today:

_____

_____

_____

_____

_____

Today I wish I could tell you:

_____

_____

_____

_____

_____

I am grateful for the time:

_____

_____

_____

_____

_____

The most difficult time of today:

_____

_____

_____

_____

Date:

_____

"Little by little we let go of loss but never of love."

Something that reminded me of you today:

_____

_____

_____

_____

_____

Today I wish I could tell you:

_____

_____

_____

_____

_____

I am grateful for the time:

_____

_____

_____

_____

_____

The most difficult time of today:

_____

_____

_____

_____

Date:

_____

"Little by little we let go of loss but never of love."

Something that reminded me of you today:

_____
_____
_____
_____
_____

Today I wish I could tell you:

_____
_____
_____
_____
_____

I am grateful for the time:

_____
_____
_____
_____
_____

The most difficult time of today:

_____
_____
_____
_____

Date:

_____

"Little by little we let go of loss but never of love."

Something that reminded me of you today:

_____
_____
_____
_____

Today I wish I could tell you:

_____
_____
_____
_____

I am grateful for the time:

_____
_____
_____
_____

The most difficult time of today:

_____
_____
_____

Date:

_____

"Little by little we let go of loss but never of love."

Something that reminded me of you today:

_____

_____

_____

_____

_____

Today I wish I could tell you:

_____

_____

_____

_____

_____

I am grateful for the time:

_____

_____

_____

_____

_____

The most difficult time of today:

_____

_____

_____

_____

Date:

_____

"Little by little we let go of loss but never of love."

Something that reminded me of you today:

_____

_____

_____

_____

Today I wish I could tell you:

_____

_____

_____

_____

I am grateful for the time:

_____

_____

_____

_____

The most difficult time of today:

_____

_____

_____

_____

Date:

_____

"Little by little we let go of loss but never of love."

Something that reminded me of you today:

_____

_____

_____

_____

Today I wish I could tell you:

_____

_____

_____

_____

I am grateful for the time:

_____

_____

_____

_____

The most difficult time of today:

_____

_____

_____

Date:

_____

"Little by little we let go of loss but never of love."

Something that reminded me of you today:

_____

_____

_____

_____

Today I wish I could tell you:

_____

_____

_____

_____

I am grateful for the time:

_____

_____

_____

_____

The most difficult time of today:

_____

_____

_____

_____

Date:

_____

"Little by little we let go of loss but never of love."

Something that reminded me of you today:

_____

_____

_____

_____

Today I wish I could tell you:

_____

_____

_____

_____

I am grateful for the time:

_____

_____

_____

_____

The most difficult time of today:

_____

_____

_____

_____

Date:
_____

"Little by little we let go of loss but never of love."

Something that reminded me of you today:

_____
_____
_____
_____

Today I wish I could tell you:

_____
_____
_____
_____

I am grateful for the time:

_____
_____
_____
_____

The most difficult time of today:

_____
_____
_____
_____

Date:
_____

"Little by little we let go of loss but never of love."

Something that reminded me of you today:

_____

_____

_____

_____

Today I wish I could tell you:

_____

_____

_____

_____

I am grateful for the time:

_____

_____

_____

_____

The most difficult time of today:

_____

_____

_____

Date:

_____

"Little by little we let go of loss but never of love."

Something that reminded me of you today:

_____
_____
_____
_____

Today I wish I could tell you:

_____
_____
_____
_____

I am grateful for the time:

_____
_____
_____
_____

The most difficult time of today:

_____
_____
_____
_____

Date:
_____

"Little by little we let go of loss but never of love."

Something that reminded me of you today:

_____
_____
_____
_____

Today I wish I could tell you:

_____
_____
_____
_____

I am grateful for the time:

_____
_____
_____
_____

The most difficult time of today:

_____
_____
_____

Date:

_____

"Little by little we let go of loss but never of love."

Something that reminded me of you today:

_____

_____

_____

_____

_____

Today I wish I could tell you:

_____

_____

_____

_____

_____

I am grateful for the time:

_____

_____

_____

_____

_____

The most difficult time of today:

_____

_____

_____

_____

Date:

_____

"Little by little we let go of loss but never of love."

Something that reminded me of you today:

_____

_____

_____

_____

Today I wish I could tell you:

_____

_____

_____

_____

I am grateful for the time:

_____

_____

_____

_____

The most difficult time of today:

_____

_____

_____

Date:

_____

"Little by little we let go of loss but never of love."

Something that reminded me of you today:

_____

_____

_____

_____

Today I wish I could tell you:

_____

_____

_____

_____

I am grateful for the time:

_____

_____

_____

_____

The most difficult time of today:

_____

_____

_____

_____

Date:

_____

"Little by little we let go of loss but never of love."

Something that reminded me of you today:

_____

_____

_____

_____

Today I wish I could tell you:

_____

_____

_____

_____

I am grateful for the time:

_____

_____

_____

_____

The most difficult time of today:

_____

_____

_____

_____

Date:
_____

"Little by little we let go of loss but never of love."

Something that reminded me of you today:

_____
_____
_____
_____

Today I wish I could tell you:

_____
_____
_____
_____

I am grateful for the time:

_____
_____
_____
_____

The most difficult time of today:

_____
_____
_____

Date:

_____

"Little by little we let go of loss but never of love."

Something that reminded me of you today:

_____

_____

_____

_____

_____

Today I wish I could tell you:

_____

_____

_____

_____

_____

I am grateful for the time:

_____

_____

_____

_____

_____

The most difficult time of today:

_____

_____

_____

_____

Made in the USA
Middletown, DE
08 July 2020